EASY GUITAR
WITH NOTES & TAB

TOP HITS OF
2020

ISBN 978-1-7051-1185-7

Visit Hal Leonard Online at
www.halleonard.com

Contact us:
Hal Leonard
7777 West Bluemound Road
Milwaukee, WI 53213
Email: info@halleonard.com

In Europe, contact:
Hal Leonard Europe Limited
42 Wigmore Street
Marylebone, London, W1U 2RN
Email: info@halleonardeurope.com

In Australia, contact:
Hal Leonard Australia Pty. Ltd.
4 Lentara Court
Cheltenham, Victoria, 3192 Australia
Email: info@halleonard.com.au

STRUM AND PICK PATTERNS

This chart contains the suggested strum and pick patterns that are referred to by number at the beginning of each song in this book. The symbols ⊓ and ∨ in the strum patterns refer to down and up strokes, respectively. The letters in the pick patterns indicate which right-hand fingers play which strings.

p = thumb
i = index finger
m = middle finger
a = ring finger

For example; Pick Pattern 2
is played: thumb - index - middle - ring

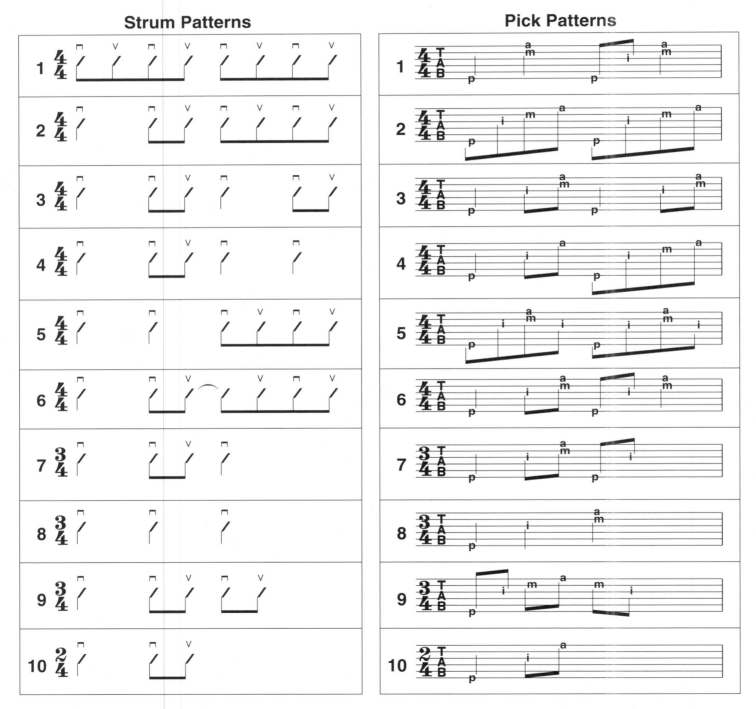

You can use the 3/4 Strum and Pick Patterns in songs written in compound meter (6/8, 9/8, 12/8, etc.).
For example, you can accompany a song in 6/8 by playing the 3/4 pattern twice in each measure.
The 4/4 Strum and Pick Patterns can be used for songs written in cut time (¢) by doubling the note
time values in the patterns. Each pattern would therefore last two measures in cut time.

Adore You

Words and Music by Harry Styles, Thomas Hull, Tyler Johnson and Amy Allen

Chorus

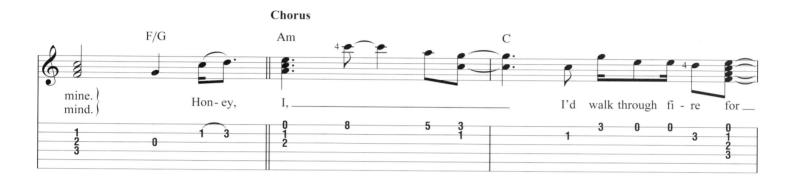

Verse

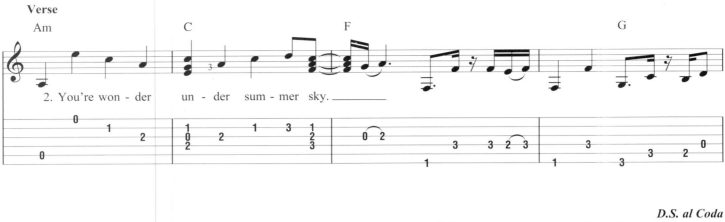

2. You're won - der un - der sum - mer sky. _____

D.S. al Coda

Brown skin and lem - on o - ver ice. _____ Would you be - lieve _ it? ____

⊕ Coda　　　　　　　　　　　**Bridge**

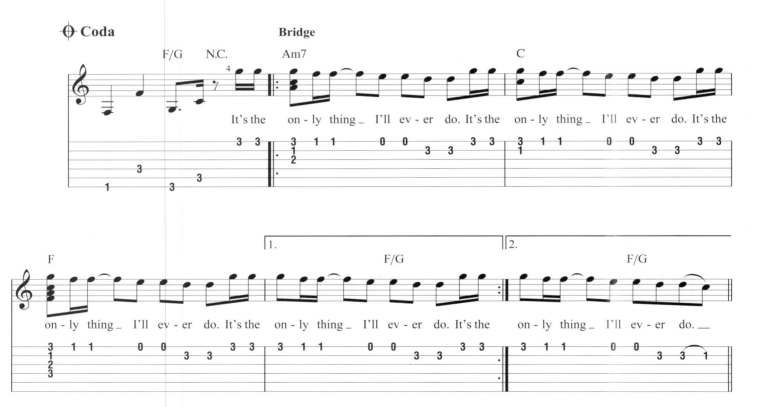

It's the on - ly thing _ I'll ev - er do. It's the on - ly thing _ I'll ev - er do. It's the

on - ly thing _ I'll ev - er do. It's the on - ly thing _ I'll ev - er do. It's the on - ly thing _ I'll ev - er do. ____

Outro-Chorus

I'd _____ walk through fi - re for ____ you. Just let me a - dore ____ you. Oh, hon - ey,

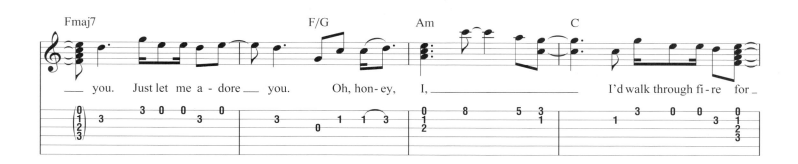

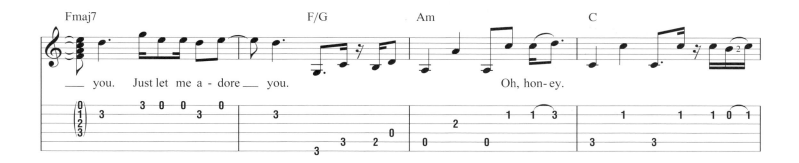

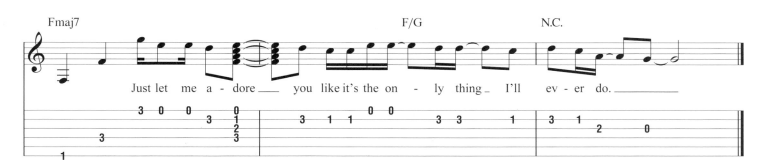

Before You Go

Words and Music by Lewis Capaldi, Benjamin Kohn, Peter Kelleher, Thomas Barnes and Philip Plested

*Capo I

Strum Pattern: 8
Pick Pattern: 8

Verse
Moderately, in 4

1. I fell by the way-side, ___ like ev'ry-one else.
2. Was nev-er the right time ___ when-ev-er you called.

"I hate you, I hate you, I
Went lit-tle by lit-tle by

*Optional: To match recording, place capo at 1st fret.
**Chord symbols reflect guitar harmony.

hate you," but I was just kid-ding my-self.
lit-tle, un-til there was noth-ing at all.

Our ev-er-y mo-ment ___
Our ev-er-y mo-ment ___

I start to re-place,
I start to re-play,

Pre-Chorus

___ 'cause now that they're gone, all I hear are the words that I need-ed to say.
___ but all I can think a-bout ___ is see-ing that look on your face.

When you hurt un-

der the sur-face, like trou-bled wa-ter run-ning cold, ___

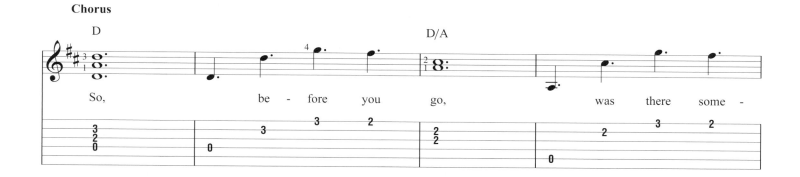

Chorus

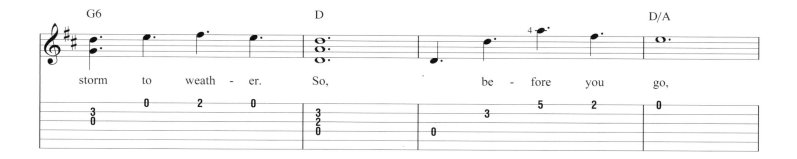

Bridge

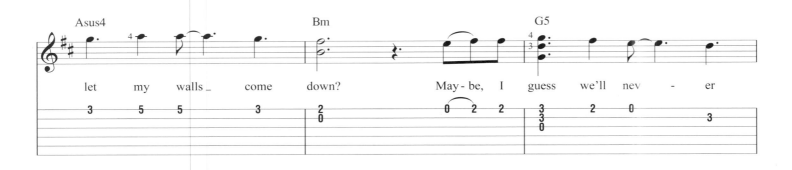

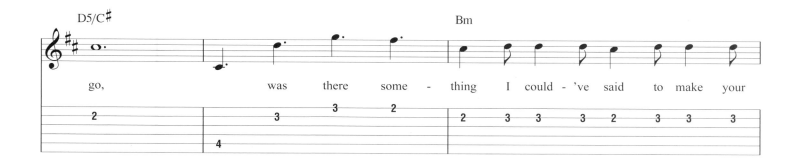

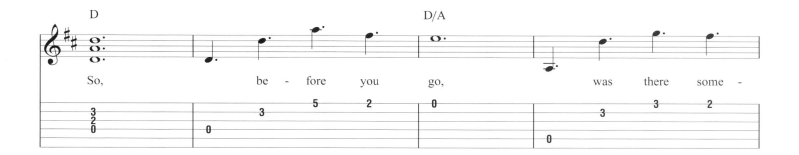

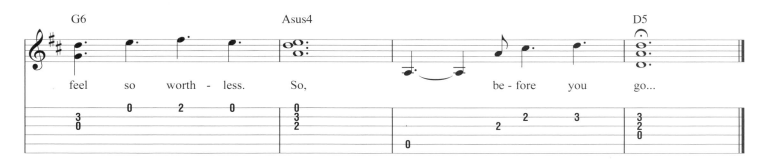

Better Days

Words and Music by Ryan Tedder, Brent Kutzle and John Nathaniel

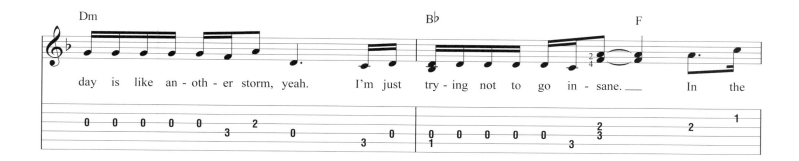

day is like an-oth-er storm, yeah. I'm just try-ing not to go in-sane.___ In the

cit - y shin-ing so bright, so man-y dark nights, so man-y dark days. But an-y-time I

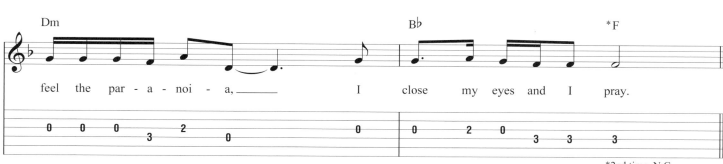

feel the par-a-noi-a,_____ I close my eyes and I pray.

*2nd time, N.C.

Chorus

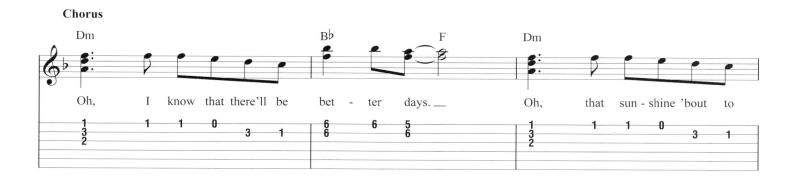

Oh, I know that there'll be bet - ter days.___ Oh, that sun-shine 'bout to

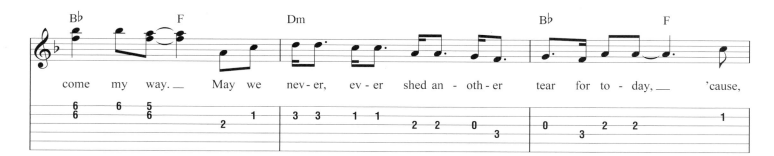

come my way.___ May we nev-er, ev-er shed an-oth-er tear for to - day,___ 'cause,

*Let chords ring till end.

Additional Lyrics

2. Been waking up to a new year;
   Got the past a million miles away.
   I've been waking up with a new fear,
   But I know it'll wash away.
   Whatever you do, don't worry 'bout me.
   I'm thinking 'bout you, don't worry 'bout us.
   'Cause in the morning, ev'rything can change, yeah,
   And time will tell you it does.

Blinding Lights

Words and Music by Abel Tesfaye, Max Martin, Jason Quenneville, Oscar Holter and Ahmad Balshe

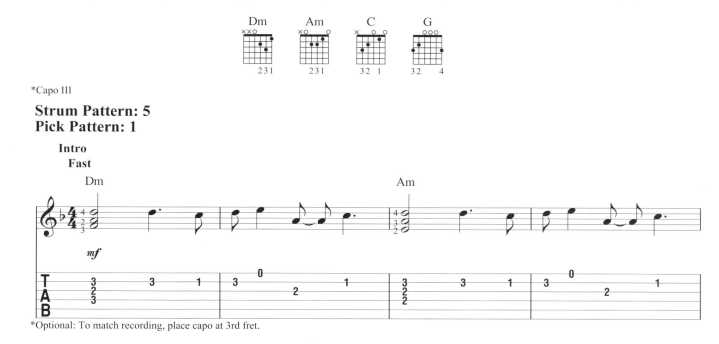

*Capo III

Strum Pattern: 5
Pick Pattern: 1

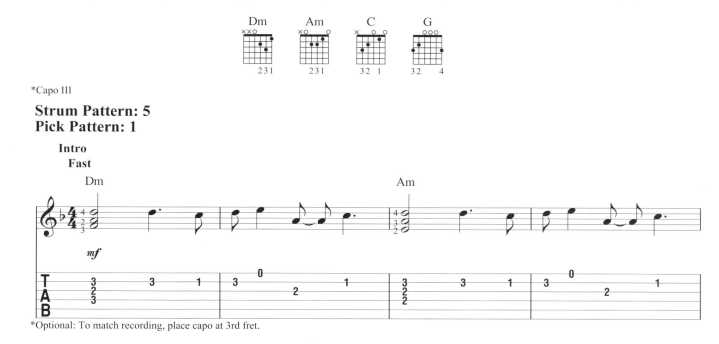

*Optional: To match recording, place capo at 3rd fret.

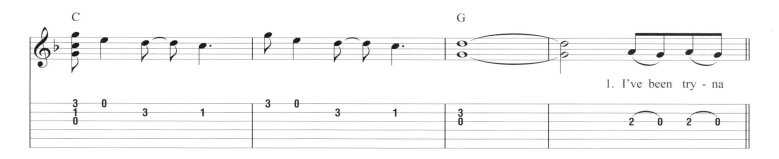

1. I've been try - na

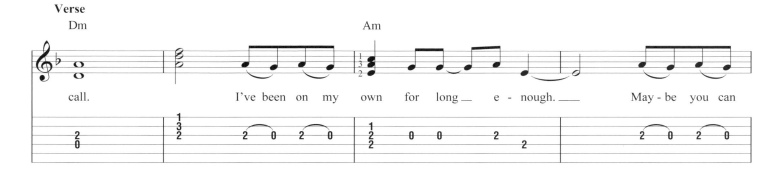

call. I've been on my own for long ___ e - nough. ___ May - be you can

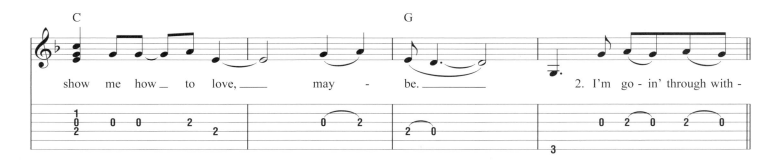

show me how ___ to love, ___ may - be. ___ 2. I'm go - in' through with -

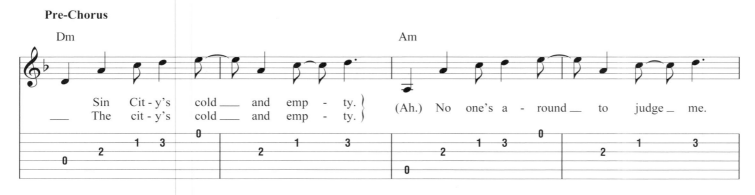

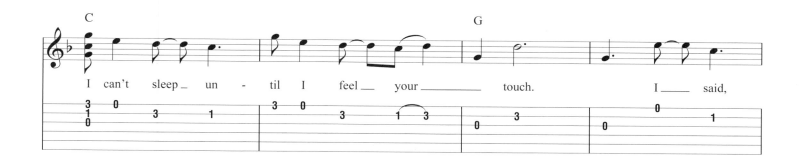

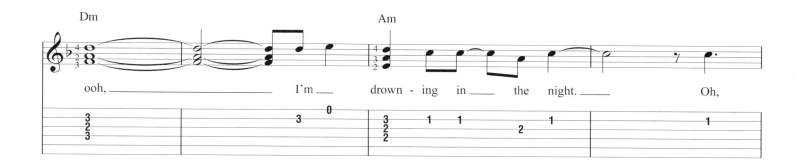

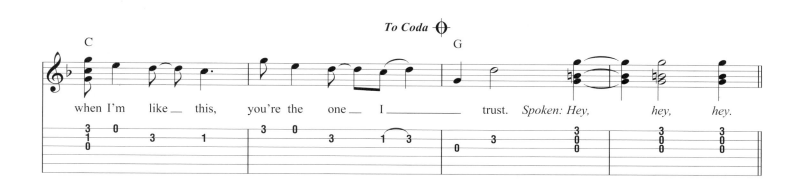

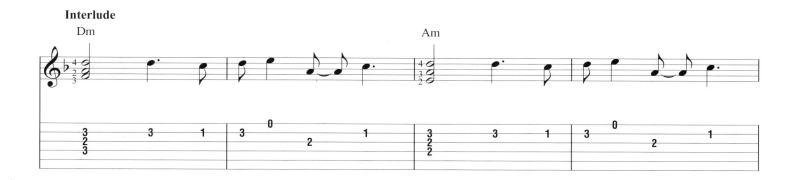

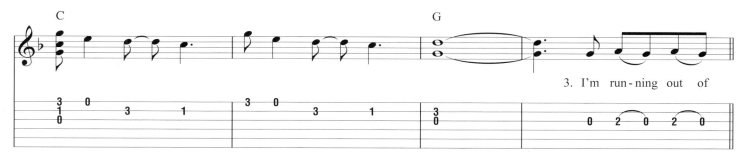

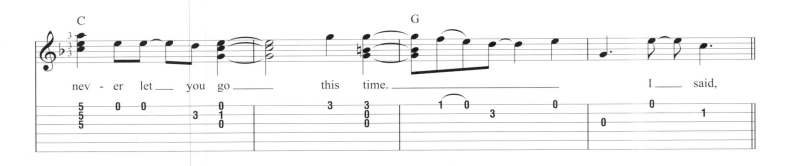

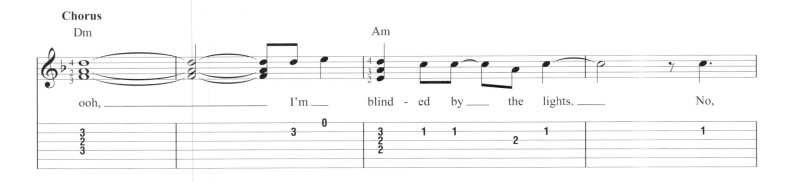

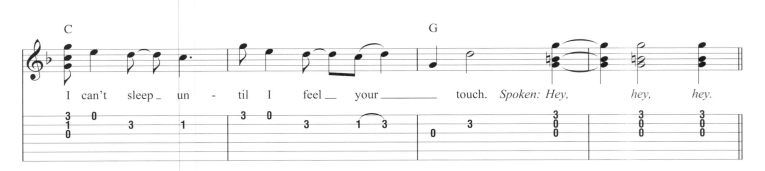

Outro

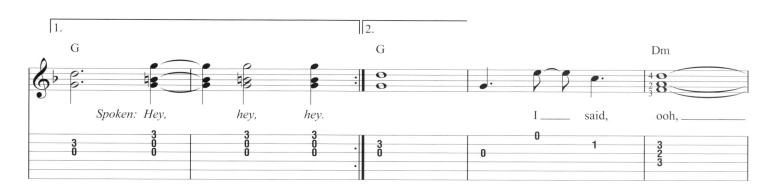

Spoken: Hey,   hey,   hey.   I ____ said,   ooh, _____

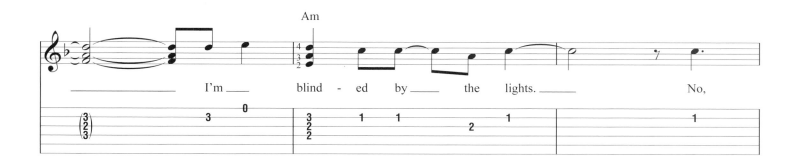

_____ I'm ____ blind - ed by ____ the lights. _____   No,

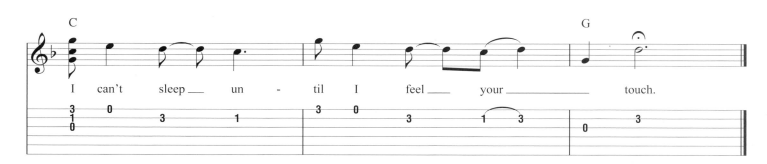

I can't sleep ____ un - til I feel ____ your _____ touch.

Cardigan

Words and Music by Taylor Swift and Aaron Dessner

Chorus

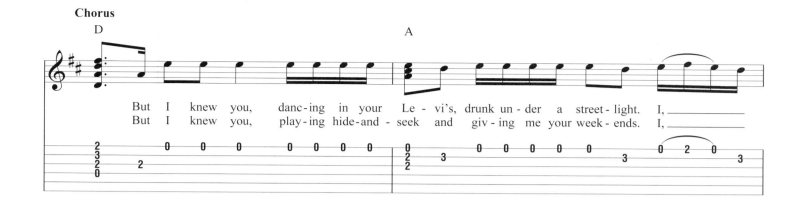

But I knew you, danc-ing in your Le - vi's, drunk un - der a street - light. I, _____
But I knew you, play-ing hide-and - seek and giv - ing me your week - ends. I, _____

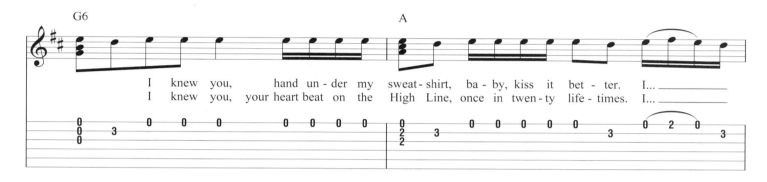

I knew you, hand un - der my sweat - shirt, ba - by, kiss it bet - ter. I... _____
I knew you, your heart beat on the High Line, once in twen - ty life - times. I... _____

1.

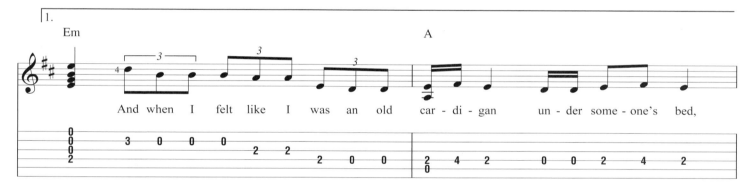

And when I felt like I was an old car - di - gan un - der some - one's bed,

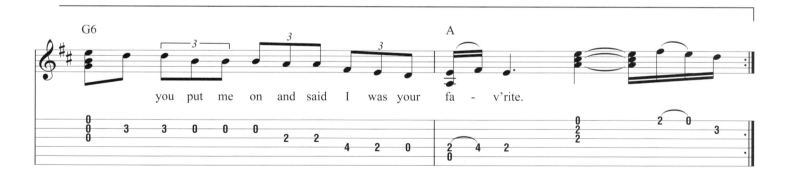

you put me on and said I was your fa - v'rite.

2.

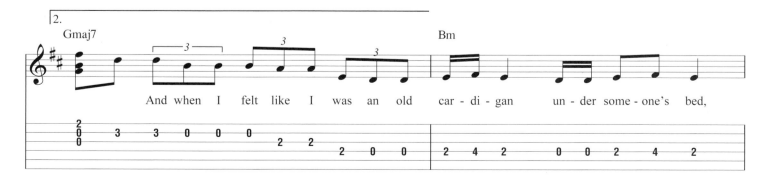

And when I felt like I was an old car - di - gan un - der some - one's bed,

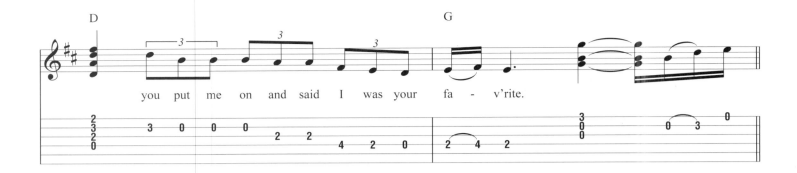

you put me on and said I was your fa - v'rite.

Bridge

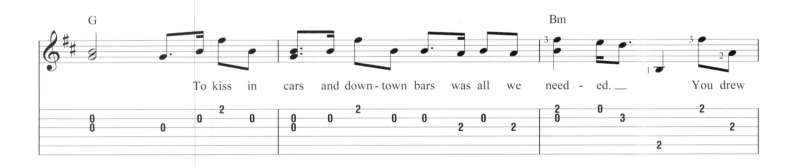

G

To kiss in cars and down-town bars was all we need - ed. ___ You drew

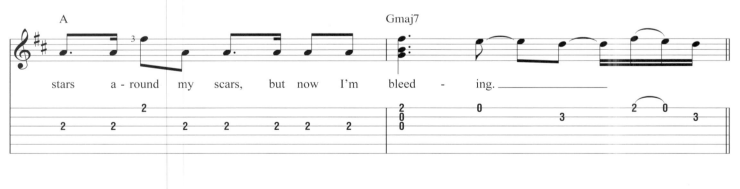

stars a - round my scars, but now I'm bleed - ing. ___

Chorus

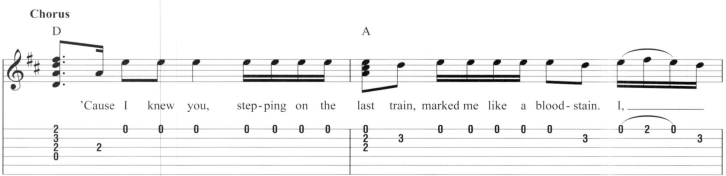

'Cause I knew you, step-ping on the last train, marked me like a blood-stain. I, ___

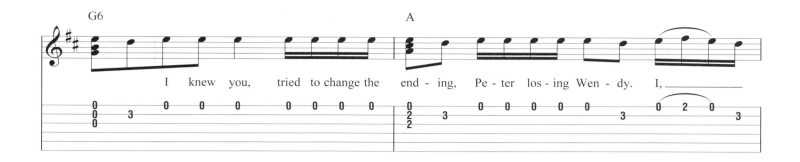

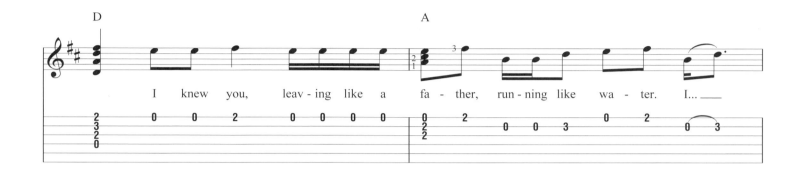

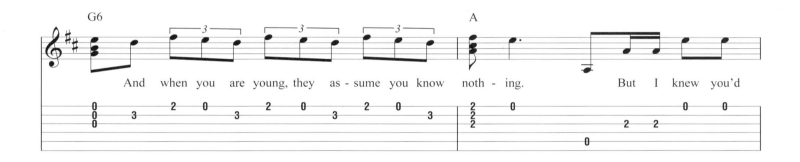

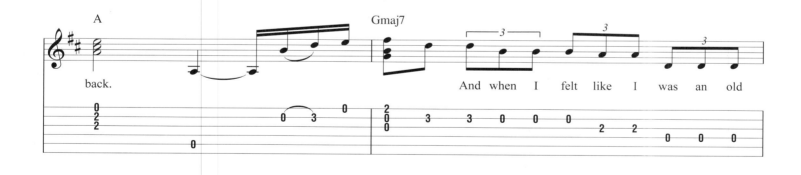

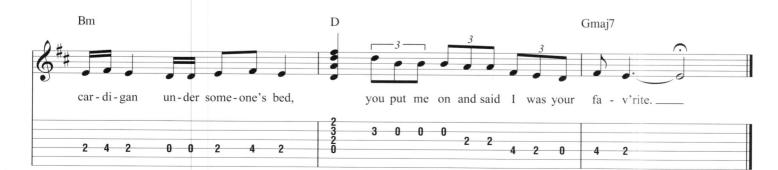

Daisies

Words and Music by Katy Perry, Michael Pollack, Jon Bellion,
Jordan Johnson, Jacob Kasher Hindlin and Stefan Johnson

*Sung as written.

Chorus

**Sung one octave higher, next 8.5 meas.

26

*Sung as written.

D.S. al Coda

Coda

Pre-Chorus

N.C.

They told me I was

*Sung one octave higher.

27

Húsavik

from the Netflix film EUROVISION SONG CONTEST - THE STORY OF FIRE SAGA

Words and Music by Rickard Göransson, Savan Kotecha and Max Grahn

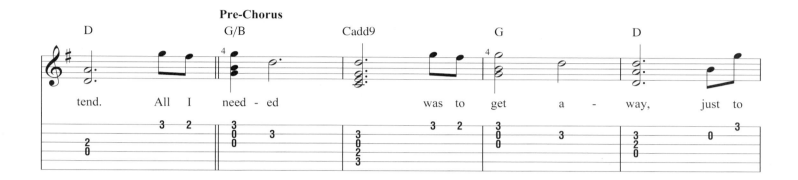

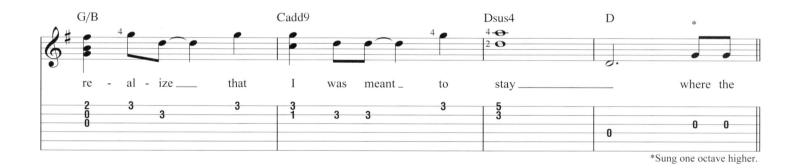

*Sung one octave higher.

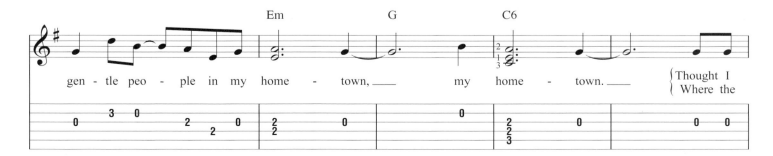

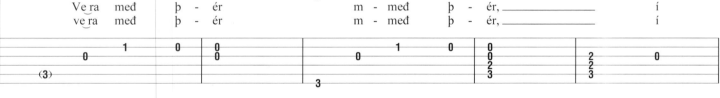

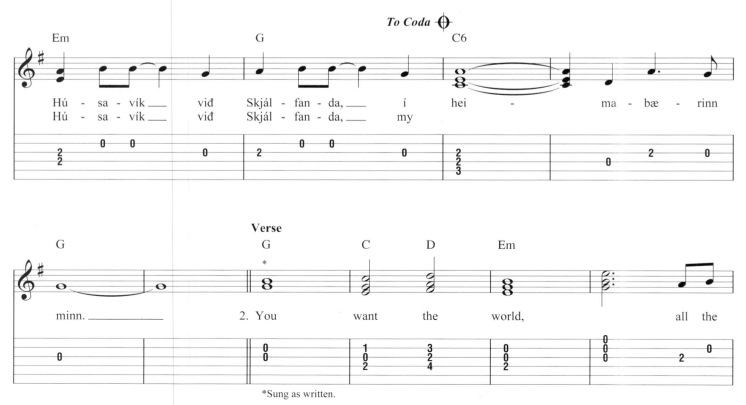

*Sung as written.

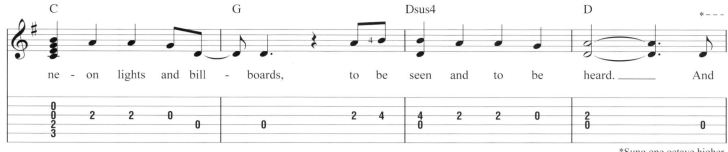

ne - on lights and bill - boards, to be seen and to be heard. _____ And

*Sung one octave higher.

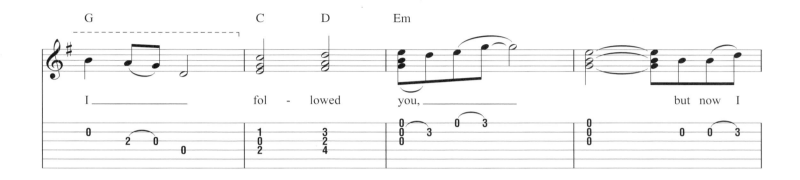

I _____ fol - lowed you, _____ but now I

D.S. al Coda

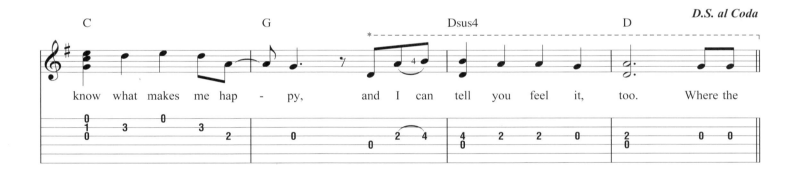

know what makes me hap - py, and I can tell you feel it, too. Where the

⊕ Coda

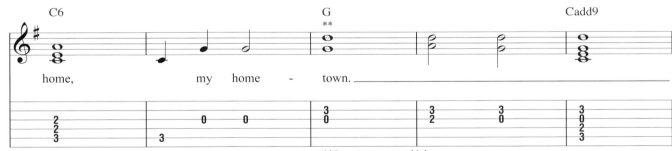

home, my home - town.

**Sung two octaves higher

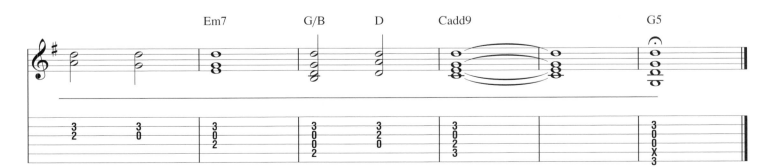

I Dare You

Words and Music by Benjamin West, Jeffrey Gitelman, Natalie Hemby, Laura Veltz and Jesse Shatkin

Pre-Chorus

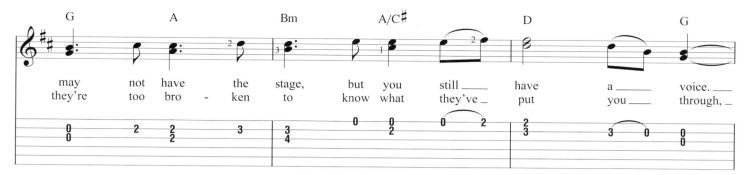

may not have the stage, but you still _____ have a _____ voice. _____
they're too bro - ken to know what they've _ put you _____ through, _

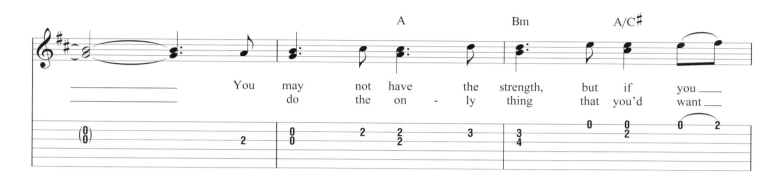

You may not have the strength, but if you _____
do the on - ly thing that you'd want _____

𝄋 Chorus

3rd time, w/ Lead Voc. ad lib.

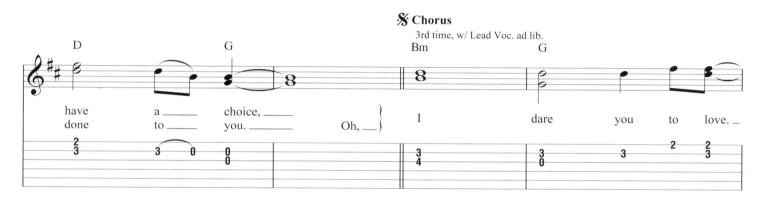

have a _____ choice, _____ Oh, _ I dare you to love. _
done to _____ you. _____

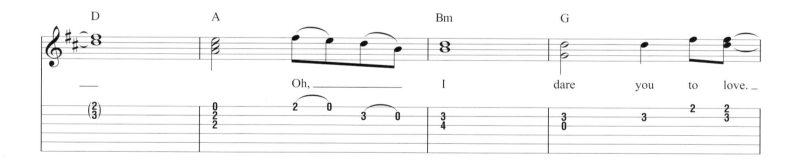

Oh, _____ I dare you to love. _

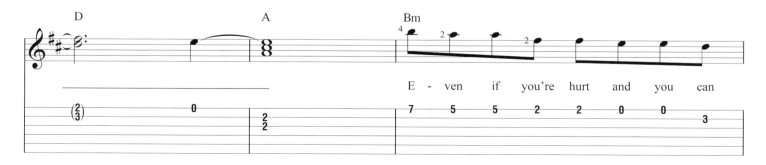

E - ven if you're hurt and you can

Interlude

*Sung one octave higher.

Pre-Chorus

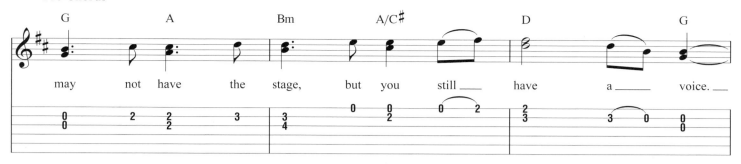

may not have the stage, but you still ___ have a ___ voice. ___

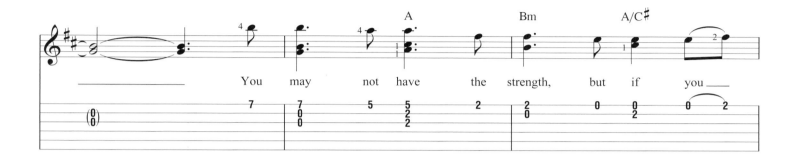

___ You may not have the strength, but if you ___

D.S. al Coda   Coda

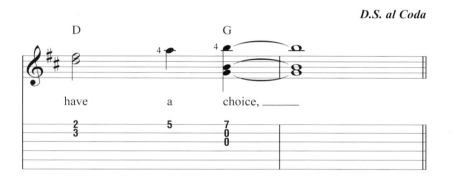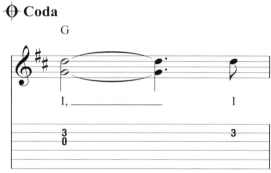

have a choice, ___   I, ___ I

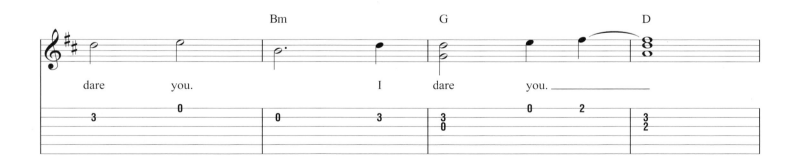

dare you. I dare you. ___

Oh, ___ I, ___ I dare you to love. ___

I'm Ready

**Words and Music by Sam Smith, Demitria Lovato, Savan Kotecha,
Anders Peter Svensson and Ilya Salmanzadeh**

*Optional: To match recording, place capo at 5th fret.

**1st time sung one octave lower.

***Sung as written.

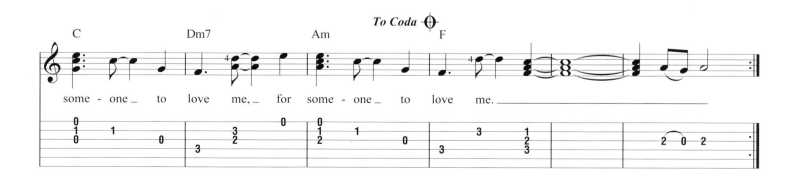

*Sung one octave lower, next 3 meas.

**Sung as written.

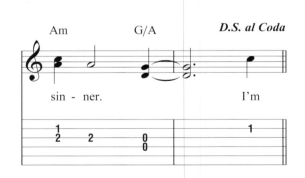

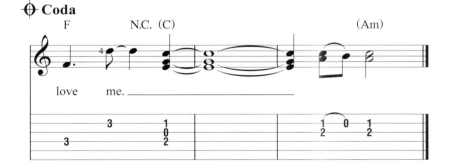

Additional Lyrics

2. It's a hot night in my head in the chill of winter.
   I've been looking hard for a lover disguised as a sinner.
   Not a cheater, a redeemer. He's a cold, cold-blooded defeater.
   It's a hot night in my head in the chill of the winter, no.

No Time to Die

from NO TIME TO DIE

Words and Music by Billie Eilish O'Connell and Finneas O'Connell

Strum Pattern: 3
Pick Pattern: 2

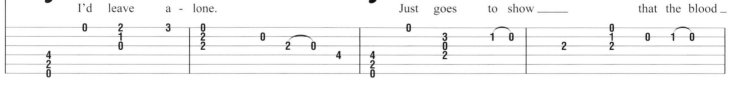

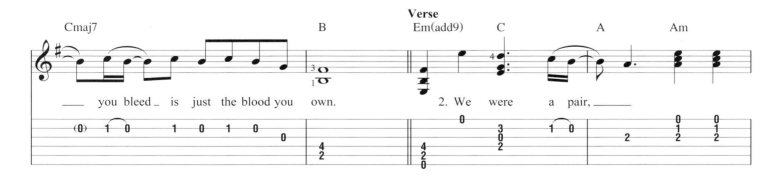

Verse

3. I let it burn _____ that you're no long-er my con-cern.

D.S. al Coda

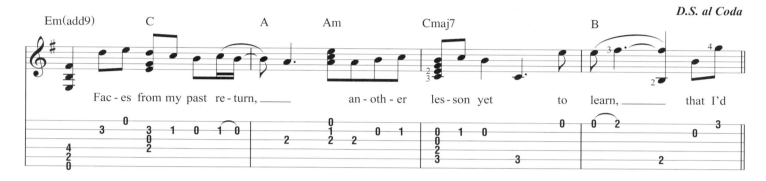

Fac-es from my past re-turn, _____ an-oth-er les-son yet to learn, _____ that I'd

Coda
Outro

No time to die. _ Hm. _____ No time to

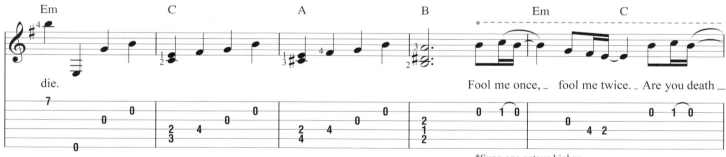

die. Fool me once, _ fool me twice. _ Are you death _

*Sung one octave higher.

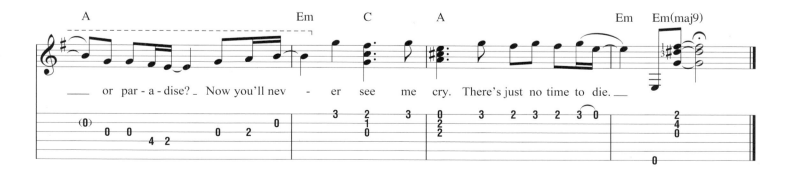

_____ or par-a-dise? _ Now you'll nev - er see me cry. There's just no time to die. _

41

Level of Concern

Words and Music by Tyler Joseph

*Sung one octave higher.

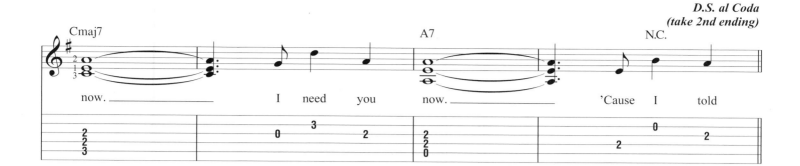

now. _____ I need you now. _____ 'Cause I told

— My lev - el of con - cern. I need you to tell me we're al - right, tell me

*Sung one octave higher.

we're o - kay. I need you. Need you. _____ Tell me. Need you. _____

**As before

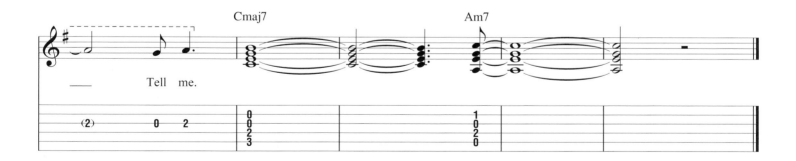

— Tell me.

Additional Lyrics

2. Panic on the brink.
Michael's gone insane.
Julie starts to make you nervous.
I don't really care what they would say.
I'm asking you to stay.
My bunker underneath the surface.
Wondering…

Nobody's Love

Words and Music by Adam Levine, Nija Charles, Jordan Johnson, Jacob Kasher Hindlin, Stefan Johnson,
Ryan Ogren, Brandon Hamlin, Rosina Russell, Michael Pollack and Kareen Lomax

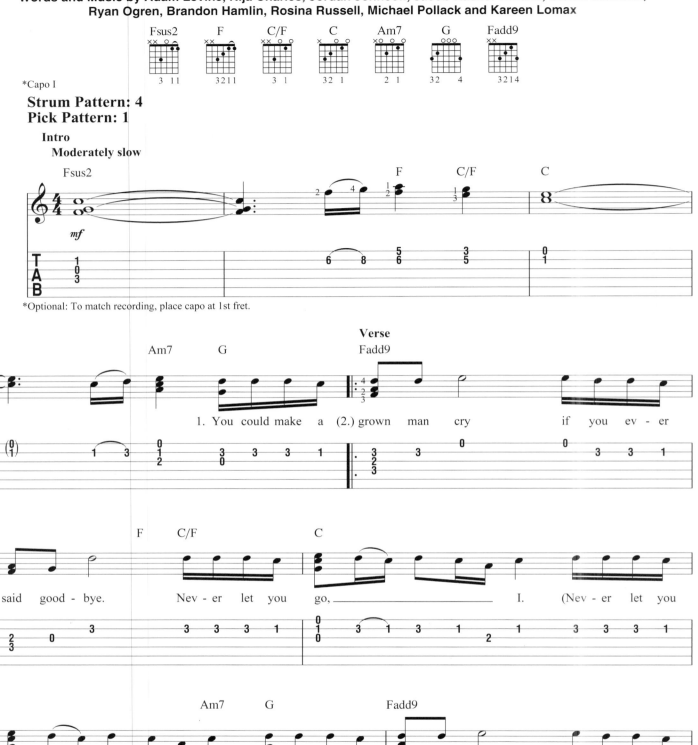

*Optional: To match recording, place capo at 1st fret.

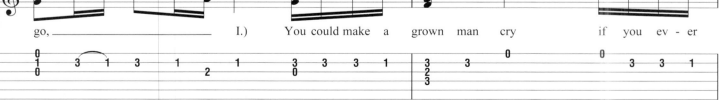

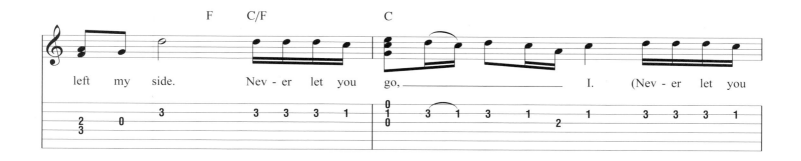

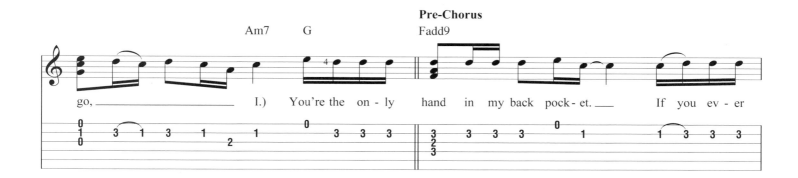

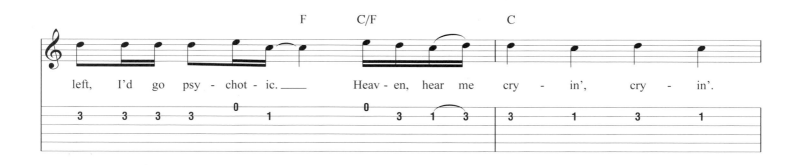

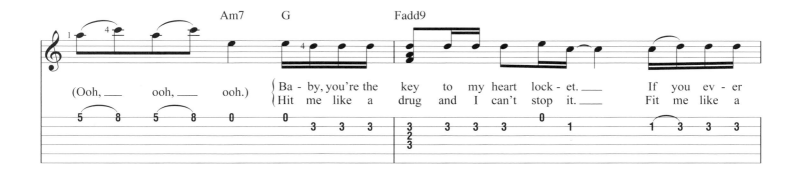

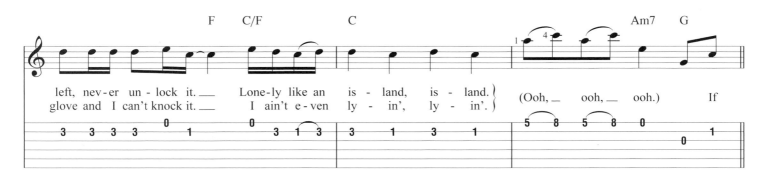

y. And if you ev-er leave, then I'm nev-er gon' want ___ no-bod-y, no-bod-y,

love. If my love ain't your love, then it's no-bod - y's. It's on-ly yours, on-ly yours, not just an-y-bod -

To Coda

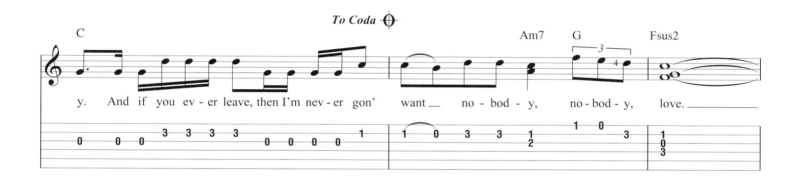

y. And if you ev-er leave, then I'm nev-er gon' want ___ no-bod - y, no-bod - y, love. ___

D.S. al Coda

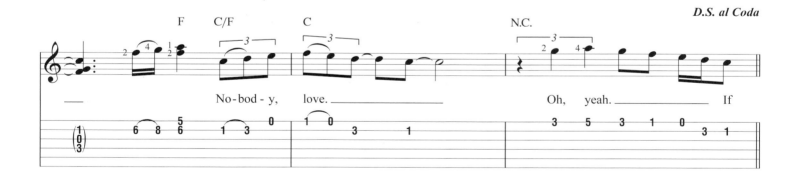

___ No-bod - y, love. ___ Oh, yeah. ___ If

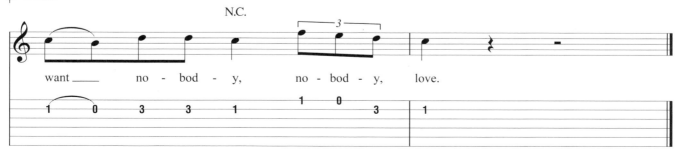

⊕ Coda

want ___ no-bod - y, no-bod - y, love.

Rain on Me

Words and Music by Stefani Germanotta, Matthew Burns, Martin Bresso,
Michael Tucker, Rami Yacoub, Ariana Grande and Nija Charles

*Optional: To match recording, place capo at 4th fret.

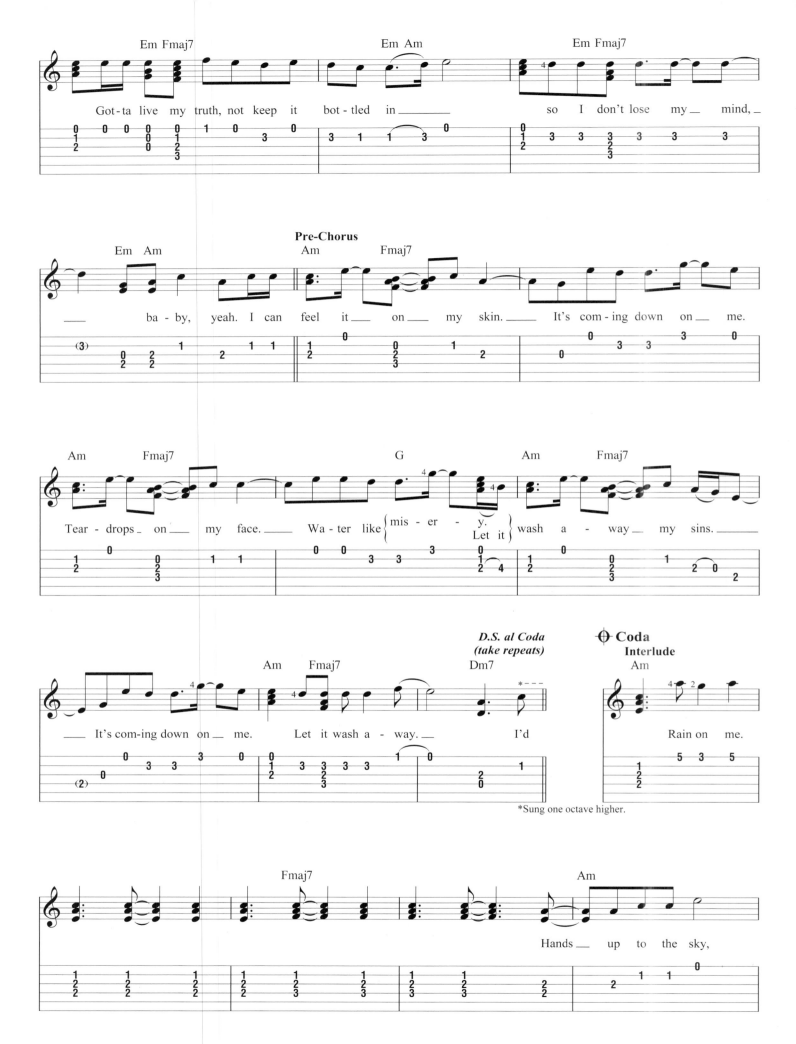

*Sung one octave higher.

One Margarita

Words and Music by Michael Carter, Matt Dragstrem and Josh Thompson

Strum Pattern: 3
Pick Pattern: 3

Intro
Moderately slow, in 2

Verse

1. Ev-'ry-bod-y here ain't ___ from here, but we're ___ here do-in' our thing. Let-

-tin' go a lit-tle, lit - tle by lit-tle, sip - pin' on a fro-zen drink. Ti-

-ki bars tik-in', pour - in' all week-end, clouds ___ ain't leak-in' no rain. Two ___

piec-es shak-in', white-caps a break-in', we ___ ain't feel-in' no pain. It goes ___ like one ___

 Chorus

mar-ga-ri - ta, two ___ mar-ga-ri - ta, three ___ mar-ga-ri - ta shot. Don't wor-

- ry 'bout to-mor-row, leave ___ all your sor - row out ___ here on the float-in' dock.

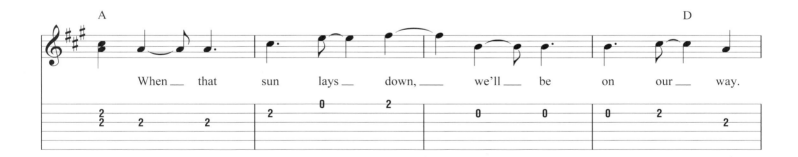

When ___ that sun lays ___ down, ___ we'll ___ be on our ___ way.

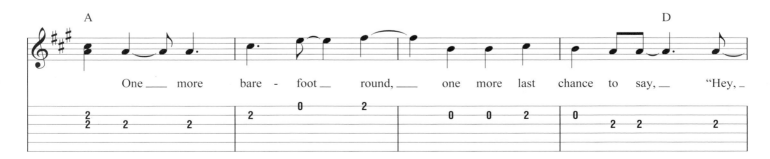

One ___ more bare - foot ___ round, ___ one more last chance to say, ___ "Hey, ___

trees a lean - in', sun - burn scream - in', but we'll all be al - right ____ af - ter one ____

⊕ Coda 1   **Guitar Solo**

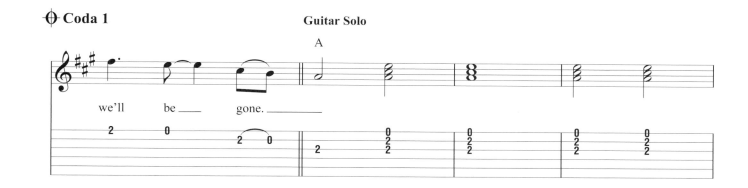

we'll be ____ gone. ____

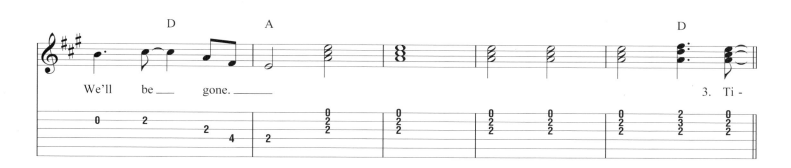

We'll be ____ gone. ____   3. Ti -

Verse
w/ Intro riff

- ki bars tik - in', pour - in' all week - end, clouds ____ ain't leak - in' no

rain.   Two ____ piec - es shak - in', white - caps a - break - in', we ____

ain't feel-in' no pain, feel-in' no pain. ____ It goes __ like one __

⊕ Coda 2

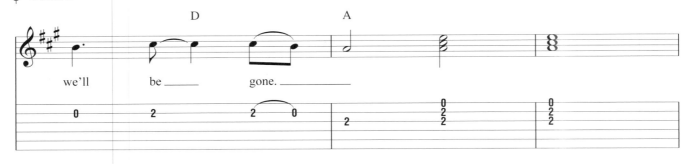

we'll be ____ gone. ____

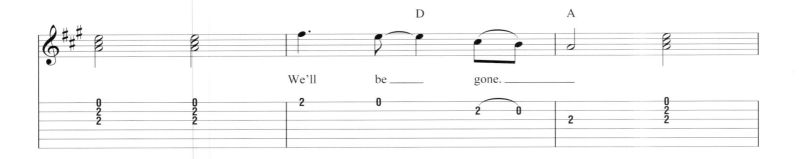

We'll be ____ gone. ____

We'll be ____ gone. ____

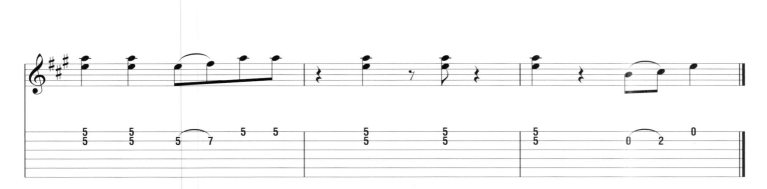

Audio Access Included

INCLUDES TAB

The **Easy Guitar Play Along**® series features streamlined transcriptions of your favorite songs. Just follow the tab, listen to the audio to hear how the guitar should sound, and then play along using the backing tracks. Playback tools are provided for slowing down the tempo without changing pitch and looping challenging parts. The melody and lyrics are included in the book so that you can sing or simply follow along.

1. ROCK CLASSICS
Jailbreak • Living After Midnight • Mississippi Queen • Rocks Off • Runnin' Down a Dream • Smoke on the Water • Strutter • Up Around the Bend.
00702560 Book/CD Pack....... $14.99

2. ACOUSTIC TOP HITS
About a Girl • I'm Yours • The Lazy Song • The Scientist • 21 Guns • Upside Down • What I Got • Wonderwall.
00702569 Book/CD Pack....... $14.99

3. ROCK HITS
All the Small Things • Best of You • Brain Stew (The Godzilla Remix) • Californication • Island in the Sun • Plush • Smells Like Teen Spirit • Use Somebody.
00702570 Book/CD Pack....... $14.99

4. ROCK 'N' ROLL
Blue Suede Shoes • I Get Around • I'm a Believer • Jailhouse Rock • Oh, Pretty Woman • Peggy Sue • Runaway • Wake Up Little Susie.
00702572 Book/CD Pack....... $14.99

6. CHRISTMAS SONGS
Have Yourself a Merry Little Christmas • A Holly Jolly Christmas • The Little Drummer Boy • Run Rudolph Run • Santa Claus Is Comin' to Town • Silver and Gold • Sleigh Ride • Winter Wonderland.
00101879 Book/CD Pack......... $14.99

7. BLUES SONGS FOR BEGINNERS
Come On (Part 1) • Double Trouble • Gangster of Love • I'm Ready • Let Me Love You Baby • Mary Had a Little Lamb • San-Ho-Zay • T-Bone Shuffle.
00103235 Book/Online Audio $14.99

8. ACOUSTIC SONGS FOR BEGINNERS
Barely Breathing • Drive • Everlong • Good Riddance (Time of Your Life) • Hallelujah • Hey There Delilah • Lake of Fire • Photograph.
00103240 Book/CD Pack $15.99

9. ROCK SONGS FOR BEGINNERS
Are You Gonna Be My Girl • Buddy Holly • Everybody Hurts • In Bloom • Otherside • The Rock Show • Santa Monica • When I Come Around.
00103255 Book/CD Pack.....$14.99

10. GREEN DAY
Basket Case • Boulevard of Broken Dreams • Good Riddance (Time of Your Life) • Holiday • Longview • 21 Guns • Wake Me up When September Ends • When I Come Around.
00122322 Book/CD Pack $14.99

11. NIRVANA
All Apologies • Come As You Are • Heart Shaped Box • Lake of Fire • Lithium • The Man Who Sold the World • Rape Me • Smells Like Teen Spirit.
00122325 Book/ Online Audio $14.99

13. AC/DC
Back in Black • Dirty Deeds Done Dirt Cheap • For Those About to Rock (We Salute You) • Hells Bells • Highway to Hell • Rock and Roll Ain't Noise Pollution • T.N.T. • You Shook Me All Night Long.
14042895 Book/ Online Audio........$16.99

14. JIMI HENDRIX – SMASH HITS
All Along the Watchtower • Can You See Me • Crosstown Traffic • Fire • Foxey Lady • Hey Joe • Manic Depression • Purple Haze • Red House • Remember • Stone Free • The Wind Cries Mary.
00130591 Book/ Online Audio........$24.99

HAL•LEONARD®
www.halleonard.com

FIRST 50

Books in the First 50 series contain easy to intermediate arrangements for must-know songs. Each arrangement is simple and streamlined, yet still captures the essence of the tune.

First 50 Bluegrass Solos You Should Play on Guitar
I Am a Man of Constant Sorrow • Long Journey Home • Molly and Tenbrooks • Old Joe Clark • Rocky Top • Salty Dog Blues • and more!
00298574 Solo Guitar **$14.99**

First 50 Blues Songs You Should Play on Guitar
All Your Love (I Miss Loving) • Bad to the Bone • Born Under a Bad Sign • Dust My Broom • Hoodoo Man Blues • Little Red Rooster • Love Struck Baby • Pride and Joy • Smoking Gun • Still Got the Blues • The Thrill Is Gone • You Shook Me • and many more.
00235790 Guitar **$14.99**

First 50 Blues Turnarounds You Should Play on Guitar
You'll learn cool turnarounds in the styles of these jazz legends: John Lee Hooker, Robert Johnson, Joe Pass, Jimmy Rogers, Hubert Sumlin, Stevie Ray Vaughan, T-Bone Walker, Muddy Waters, and more!
00277469 Guitar **$14.99**

First 50 Chords You Should Play on Guitar
American Pie • Back in Black • Brown Eyed Girl • Landslide • Let It Be • Riptide • Summer of '69 • Take Me Home, Country Roads • Won't Get Fooled Again • You've Got a Friend • and more.
00300255 Guitar **$12.99**

First 50 Classical Pieces You Should Play on Guitar
This collection includes compositions by J.S. Bach, Augustin Barrios, Matteo Carcassi, Domenico Scarlatti, Fernando Sor, Francisco Tárrega, Robert de Visée, Antonio Vivaldi and many more.
00155414 Solo Guitar **$14.99**

First 50 Folk Songs You Should Play on Guitar
Amazing Grace • Down by the Riverside • Home on the Range • I've Been Working on the Railroad • Kumbaya • Man of Constant Sorrow • Oh! Susanna • This Little Light of Mine • When the Saints Go Marching In • The Yellow Rose of Texas • and more.
00235868 Guitar **$14.99**

First 50 Jazz Standards You Should Play on Guitar
All the Things You Are • Body and Soul • Don't Get Around Much Anymore • Fly Me to the Moon (In Other Words) • The Girl from Ipanema (Garota De Ipanema) • I Got Rhythm • Laura • Misty • Night and Day • Satin
00198594 Solo Guitar **$14.99**

First 50 Kids' Songs You Should Play on Guitar
Do-Re-Mi • Hakuna Matata • Let It Go • My Favorite Things • Puff the Magic Dragon • Take Me Out to the Ball Game • Won't You Be My Neighbor? (It's a Beautiful Day in the Neighborhood) • and more.
00300500 Guitar **$14.99**

First 50 Licks You Should Play on Guitar
Licks presented include the styles of legendary guitarists like Eric Clapton, Buddy Guy, Jimi Hendrix, B.B. King, Randy Rhoads, Carlos Santana, Stevie Ray Vaughan and many more.
00278875 Book/Online Audio **$14.99**

First 50 Riffs You Should Play on Guitar
All Right Now • Back in Black • Barracuda • Carry on Wayward Son • Crazy Train • La Grange • Layla • Seven Nation Army • Smoke on the Water • Sunday Bloody Sunday • Sunshine of Your Love • Sweet Home Alabama • Working Man • and more!
00277366 Guitar **$12.99**

First 50 Rock Songs You Should Play on Electric Guitar
All Along the Watchtower • Beat It • Brown Eyed Girl • Cocaine • Detroit Rock City • Hallelujah • (I Can't Get No) Satisfaction • Oh, Pretty Woman • Pride and Joy • Seven Nation Army • Should I Stay or Should I Go • Smells like Teen Spirit • Smoke on the Water • When I Come Around • You Really Got Me • and more.
00131159 Guitar **$14.99**

First 50 Songs You Should Fingerpick on Guitar
Annie's Song • Blackbird • The Boxer • Classical Gas • Dust in the Wind • Fire and Rain • Greensleeves • Road Trippin' • Shape of My Heart • Tears in Heaven • Time in a Bottle • Vincent (Starry Starry Night) • and more.
00149269 Solo Guitar **$14.99**

First 50 Songs You Should Play on 12-String Guitar
California Dreamin' • Closer to the Heart • Free Fallin' • Give a Little Bit • Hotel California • Leaving on a Jet Plane • Life by the Drop • Over the Hills and Far Away • Solsbury Hill • Space Oddity • Wish You Were Here • You Wear It Well • and more!
00287559 Guitar **$14.99**

First 50 Songs You Should Play on Acoustic Guitar
Against the Wind • Boulevard of Broken Dreams • Champagne Supernova • Every Rose Has Its Thorn • Fast Car • Free Fallin' • Layla • Let Her Go • Mean • One • Ring of Fire • Signs • Stairway to Heaven • Trouble • Wagon Wheel • Yellow • Yesterday • and more.
00131209 Guitar **$14.99**

First 50 Songs You Should Play on Bass
Blister in the Sun • I Got You (I Feel Good) • Livin' on a Prayer • Low Rider • Money • Monkey Wrench • My Generation • Roxanne • Should I Stay or Should I Go • Uptown Funk • What's Going On • With or Without You • Yellow • and more!
00149189 Bass Tab Arrangements **$14.99**

First 50 Songs You Should Play on Solo Guitar
Africa • All of Me • Blue Skies • California Dreamin' • Change the World • Crazy • Dream a Little Dream of Me • Every Breath You Take • Hallelujah • Wonderful Tonight • Yesterday • You Raise Me Up • Your Song • and more.
00288843 Guitar **$14.99**

First 50 Songs You Should Strum on Guitar
American Pie • Blowin' in the Wind • Daughter • Hey, Soul Sister • Home • I Will Wait • Losing My Religion • Mrs. Robinson • No Woman No Cry • Peaceful Easy Feeling • Rocky Mountain High • Sweet Caroline • Teardrops on My Guitar • Wonderful Tonight • and more.
00148996 Guitar **$14.99**

Prices, contents and availability subject to change without notice.

www.halleonard.com

0220
014

THE BOOK SERIES

FOR EASY GUITAR

THE ACOUSTIC BOOK
00702251 Easy Guitar....................................$16.99

THE BEATLES BOOK
00699266 Easy Guitar....................................$19.95

THE BLUES BOOK – 2ND ED.
00702104 Easy Guitar....................................$16.95

THE CHRISTMAS CAROLS BOOK
00702186 Easy Guitar....................................$14.95

THE CHRISTMAS CLASSICS BOOK
00702200 Easy Guitar....................................$14.95

THE ERIC CLAPTON BOOK
00702056 Easy Guitar....................................$18.95

THE CLASSIC COUNTRY BOOK
00702018 Easy Guitar....................................$19.99

THE CLASSIC ROCK BOOK
00698977 Easy Guitar....................................$19.95

THE CONTEMPORARY CHRISTIAN BOOK
00702195 Easy Guitar....................................$17.99

THE COUNTRY CLASSIC FAVORITES BOOK
00702238 Easy Guitar $19.99

HAL•LEONARD®
www.halleonard.com

Prices, contents, and availability
subject to change without notice.

Disney characters and artwork © Disney Enterprises, Inc.

THE DISNEY SONGS BOOK
00702168 Easy Guitar....................................$19.95

THE FOLKSONGS BOOK
00702180 Easy Guitar....................................$15.99

THE GOSPEL SONGS BOOK
00702157 Easy Guitar....................................$16.99

THE HYMN BOOK
00702142 Easy Guitar....................................$14.99

THE ELVIS BOOK
00702163 Easy Guitar....................................$19.95

THE ROCK CLASSICS BOOK
00702055 Easy Guitar....................................$19.99

THE WORSHIP BOOK
00702247 Easy Guitar....................................$15.99

0717

EASY GUITAR WITH NOTES & TAB

This series features simplified arrangements with notes, tab, chord charts, and strum and pick patterns.

MIXED FOLIOS

00702287	Acoustic	$16.99
00702002	Acoustic Rock Hits for Easy Guitar	$15.99
00702166	All-Time Best Guitar Collection	$19.99
00702232	Best Acoustic Songs for Easy Guitar	$14.99
00119835	Best Children's Songs	$16.99
00702233	Best Hard Rock Songs	$15.99
00703055	The Big Book of Nursery Rhymes & Children's Songs	$16.99
00698978	Big Christmas Collection	$17.99
00702394	Bluegrass Songs for Easy Guitar	$12.99
00289632	Bohemian Rhapsody	$17.99
00703387	Celtic Classics	$14.99
00224808	Chart Hits of 2016-2017	$14.99
00267383	Chart Hits of 2017-2018	$14.99
00334293	Chart Hits of 2019-2020	$16.99
00702149	Children's Christian Songbook	$9.99
00702028	Christmas Classics	$8.99
00101779	Christmas Guitar	$14.99
00702185	Christmas Hits	$10.99
00702141	Classic Rock	$8.95
00159642	Classical Melodies	$12.99
00253933	Disney/Pixar's Coco	$16.99
00702203	CMT's 100 Greatest Country Songs	$29.99
00702283	The Contemporary Christian Collection	$16.99
00196954	Contemporary Disney	$19.99

00702239	Country Classics for Easy Guitar	$22.99
00702257	Easy Acoustic Guitar Songs	$14.99
00702280	Easy Guitar Tab White Pages	$29.99
00702041	Favorite Hymns for Easy Guitar	$10.99
00222701	Folk Pop Songs	$14.99
00126894	Frozen	$14.99
00333922	Frozen 2	$14.99
00702286	Glee	$16.99
00702160	The Great American Country Songbook	$16.99
00267383	Great American Gospel for Guitar	$12.99
00702050	Great Classical Themes for Easy Guitar	$8.99
00702116	Greatest Hymns for Guitar	$10.99
00275088	The Greatest Showman	$17.99
00148030	Halloween Guitar Songs	$14.99
00702273	Irish Songs	$12.99
00192503	Jazz Classics for Easy Guitar	$14.99
00702275	Jazz Favorites for Easy Guitar	$15.99
00702274	Jazz Standards for Easy Guitar	$17.99
00702162	Jumbo Easy Guitar Songbook	$19.99
00232285	La La Land	$16.99
00702258	Legends of Rock	$14.99
00702189	MTV's 100 Greatest Pop Songs	$24.95
00702272	1950s Rock	$15.99
00702271	1960s Rock	$15.99
00702270	1970s Rock	$16.99
00702269	1980s Rock	$15.99

00702268	1990s Rock	$19.99
00109725	Once	$14.99
00702187	Selections from O Brother Where Art Thou?	$19.99
00702178	100 Songs for Kids	$14.99
00702515	Pirates of the Caribbean	$16.99
00702125	Praise and Worship for Guitar	$10.99
00287930	Songs from A Star Is Born, The Greatest Showman, La La Land, and More Movie Musicals	$16.99
00702285	Southern Rock Hits	$12.99
00156420	Star Wars Music	$14.99
00121535	30 Easy Celtic Guitar Solos	$15.99
00702156	3-Chord Rock	$12.99
00702220	Today's Country Hits	$12.99
00244654	Top Hits of 2017	$14.99
00283786	Top Hits of 2018	$14.99
00702294	Top Worship Hits	$15.99
00702255	VH1's 100 Greatest Hard Rock Songs	$29.99
00702175	VH1's 100 Greatest Songs of Rock and Roll	$27.99
00702253	Wicked	$12.99

ARTIST COLLECTIONS

00702267	AC/DC for Easy Guitar	$15.99
00702598	Adele for Easy Guitar	$15.99
00156221	Adele – 25	$16.99
00702040	Best of the Allman Brothers	$16.99
00702865	J.S. Bach for Easy Guitar	$14.99
00702169	Best of The Beach Boys	$12.99
00702292	The Beatles — 1	$19.99
00125796	Best of Chuck Berry	$15.99
00702201	The Essential Black Sabbath	$12.95
00702250	blink-182 — Greatest Hits	$16.99
02501615	Zac Brown Band — The Foundation	$19.99
02501621	Zac Brown Band — You Get What You Give	$16.99
00702043	Best of Johnny Cash	$16.99
00702090	Eric Clapton's Best	$12.99
00702086	Eric Clapton — from the Album Unplugged	$15.99
00702202	The Essential Eric Clapton	$15.99
00702053	Best of Patsy Cline	$15.99
00222697	Very Best of Coldplay – 2nd Edition	$14.99
00702229	The Very Best of Creedence Clearwater Revival	$15.99
00702145	Best of Jim Croce	$15.99
00702219	David Crowder*Band Collection	$12.95
00702278	Crosby, Stills & Nash	$12.99
14042809	Bob Dylan	$14.99
00702276	Fleetwood Mac — Easy Guitar Collection	$16.99
00139462	The Very Best of Grateful Dead	$15.99
00702136	Best of Merle Haggard	$14.99
00702227	Jimi Hendrix — Smash Hits	$19.99
00702288	Best of Hillsong United	$12.99
00702236	Best of Antonio Carlos Jobim	$15.99

00702245	Elton John — Greatest Hits 1970–2002	$17.99
00129855	Jack Johnson	$16.99
00702204	Robert Johnson	$12.99
00702234	Selections from Toby Keith — 35 Biggest Hits	$12.95
00702003	Kiss	$16.99
00110578	Best of Kutless	$12.99
00702216	Lynyrd Skynyrd	$16.99
00702182	The Essential Bob Marley	$14.99
00146081	Maroon 5	$14.99
00121925	Bruno Mars – Unorthodox Jukebox	$12.99
00702248	Paul McCartney — All the Best	$14.99
00702129	Songs of Sarah McLachlan	$12.95
00125484	The Best of MercyMe	$12.99
02501316	Metallica — Death Magnetic	$19.99
00702209	Steve Miller Band — Young Hearts (Greatest Hits)	$12.95
00124167	Jason Mraz	$15.99
00702096	Best of Nirvana	$15.99
00702211	The Offspring — Greatest Hits	$12.95
00138026	One Direction	$14.99
00702030	Best of Roy Orbison	$16.99
00702144	Best of Ozzy Osbourne	$14.99
00702279	Tom Petty	$12.99
00102911	Pink Floyd	$16.99
00702139	Elvis Country Favorites	$17.99
00702293	The Very Best of Prince	$16.99
00699415	Best of Queen for Guitar	$15.99
00109279	Best of R.E.M.	$14.99
00702208	Red Hot Chili Peppers — Greatest Hits	$16.99
00198960	The Rolling Stones	$16.99
00174793	The Very Best of Santana	$14.99
00702196	Best of Bob Seger	$15.99

00146046	Ed Sheeran	$17.99
00702252	Frank Sinatra — Nothing But the Best	$17.99
00702010	Best of Rod Stewart	$16.99
00702049	Best of George Strait	$14.99
00702259	Taylor Swift for Easy Guitar	$15.99
00254499	Taylor Swift – Easy Guitar Anthology	$19.99
00702260	Taylor Swift — Fearless	$14.99
00139727	Taylor Swift — 1989	$17.99
00115960	Taylor Swift — Red	$16.99
00253667	Taylor Swift — Reputation	$17.99
00702290	Taylor Swift — Speak Now	$16.99
00702223	Chris Tomlin—Arriving	$16.99
00232849	Chris Tomlin Collection – 2nd Edition	$12.95
00702226	Chris Tomlin — See the Morning	$12.95
00148643	Train	$14.99
00702427	U2 — 18 Singles	$16.99
00702108	Best of Stevie Ray Vaughan	$16.99
00279005	The Who	$14.99
00702123	Best of Hank Williams	$15.99
00194548	Best of John Williams	$14.99
00702111	Stevie Wonder — Guitar Collection	$9.95
00702228	Neil Young — Greatest Hits	$15.99
00119133	Neil Young — Harvest	$14.99

Prices, contents and availability subject to change without notice.

HAL•LEONARD®

Visit Hal Leonard online at **halleonard.com**